Property Of
Cardington-Lincoln Public Library

CHRISTOPHER CHURCHMOUSE CLASSICS®

THE SHINY RED SLED

"Be gentle and ready to forgive; never hold grudges. Remember, the Lord forgave you, so you must forgive others" —Colossians 3:13.

WRITTEN BY BARBARA DAVOLL
Pictures by Dennis Hockerman

A Sonflower Book

VICTOR BOOKS®
A DIVISION OF SCRIPTURE PRESS PUBLICATIONS INC.
USA CANADA ENGLAND

Property Of
Cardington-Lincoln Public Library

RAC - 40

CHRISTOPHER CHURCHMOUSE CLASSICS

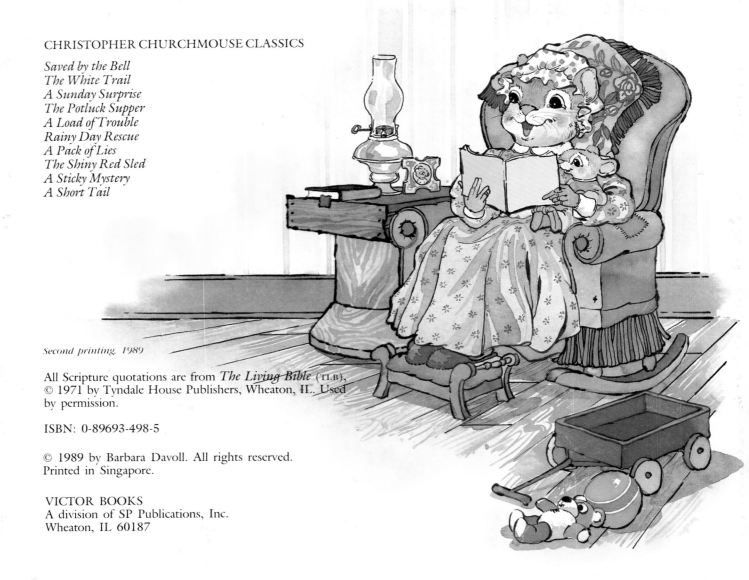

Second printing, 1989

All Scripture quotations are from *The Living Bible* (TLB),
© 1971 by Tyndale House Publishers, Wheaton, IL. Used
by permission.

ISBN: 0-89693-498-5

© 1989 by Barbara Davoll. All rights reserved.
Printed in Singapore.

VICTOR BOOKS
A division of SP Publications, Inc.
Wheaton, IL 60187

A Word to Parents and Teachers

The Christopher Churchmouse Classics will please both the eyes and ears of children, and help them grow in the knowledge of God.

This book, *The Shiny Red Sled,* one of the character-building stories in the series, is about quarreling.

"Be gentle and ready to forgive; never hold grudges. Remember, the Lord forgave you, so you must forgive others"
—Colossians 3:13 (TLB).

Through this story about Christopher, children will see a practical application of this Bible truth.

Use the Discussion Starters on page 24 to help children remember the story and the valuable lesson it teaches. Happy reading!

Christopher's Friend,

Barbara Davoll

Christopher Churchmouse gave one final tug to his boot. "There," he said. "I didn't think I'd ever get that on. Mama, do I really have to wear all these clothes?" he asked, standing up. "I can hardly move. How am I going to slide down the hill?"

Mama laughed at him. "You'll be glad for all that warm clothing when you go outside, Christopher. It is very snowy and cold. Be sure to keep that scarf wrapped tightly around your neck."

"Yes, Mama." Giving her a quick kiss, Christopher scooted out the door and into the hall where his friend, Freddie Fieldmouse, was waiting.

"Just a minute, Freddie. Let me get my sled. Isn't she a beauty?" asked Christopher, getting his new red sled from behind the door. "Look at these runners!" he exclaimed, pointing to the two gleaming strips of metal underneath the seat.

"It's a beauty, all right," responded Freddie. "No one else has one like it."

5

Soon the boys were on their way, pulling the sled behind them, out to a little hill behind the church. Chris and Freddie could hear the other mice children squeaking and squealing excitedly. They were sliding down the little mound of snow on anything they could find. Some were sliding in matchboxes, some in jar lids, and some on different types of sleds.

"Look at Ted sliding in that bottle cap," laughed Christopher, pointing at his cousin, who was twisting and

twirling down the little slope. Across the way some of the other cousins were trying out some new matchstick skis.

"This is sure going to be a fun day," said Freddie.

"I'll say."

When Christopher and Freddie reached the top of the hill, Christopher flopped onto the sled, and away he went, down the hill.

He drew in his breath sharply. What fun it was flying over the snow. He'd never gone so fast in all of his life. Crashing into the soft snow at the bottom of the hill, Christopher dusted himself off and trudged back up to the top.

"OK, Freddie, it's your turn now. Wow, is it fast! Be careful with the sled."

Freddie zoomed down the hill and fell into the soft snow, laughing.

"Hey, Chris, this is really fun!" Freddie shouted.

Soon Christopher's cousins all lined up to take their turns on the sled. The morning went by so quickly Christopher and Freddie could hardly believe it was time for lunch.

Just as the boys were starting to leave the slope, Christopher's cousin Ted said, "Hey, Chris, how about leaving your sled out here while you go in for lunch?"

9

"Oh, I don't know, Ted. I don't think I should. Something might happen to it."

"I'm your cousin, aren't I? I'm going to watch out for your sled. I won't let anything happen to it. I've been careful so far, haven't I?"

"Yes, Ted, but I think I ought to take it in with me."

About that time another cousin, Sed, spoke up.

"Come on, Chris, be a sport. Leave it out here. You know the rest of us don't have a new sled."

"Well, all right," said Christopher, handing the rope to Ted. "Do you promise to take good care of it?"

"You can count on me," said Ted.

After lunch when Chris and Freddie went back outside, they noticed that Christopher's red sled was at the bottom of the little slope. Several of the mice children were standing around it.

"Hey, what's going on?" shouted Christopher.

Sed shouted, "Hey, Chris—Ted put a big scratch on your new sled!"

"It wasn't my fault," said Ted, puffing over to Freddie and Christopher.

11

"It was too!" cried Sed angrily. "It was *your* fault we hit that tree!"

"I didn't mean to, Christopher. I really didn't mean to," said Ted.

"Let me see the sled," demanded Christopher.

Sure enough, the new sled had a great big scratch. "Oh, Ted—how could you?" said Christopher in despair. "I trusted you. You said you would take care of my sled! How could you do such a thing?"

"I didn't mean to, Christopher. It was just that we were going so fast—and the tree was there—and I tried to go around it—but we hit it. I really didn't mean to," Ted moaned, hanging his head and biting his lip.

"My sled is ruined." Christopher was almost ready to cry.

"It's not ruined," Ted insisted. "It's just scratched. It will still run."

"I know, but it's not new-looking anymore. Oh, I should never have let you borrow it, Ted. I knew I shouldn't have left it with you."

"Well, why did you then?" yelled Ted. "I'm sorry I borrowed it at all. You can just have your old sled!" With that Ted kicked the sled and stomped off.

13

"Can you believe him?" exclaimed Christopher in disgust. "He puts a big scratch on *my* sled and now he's mad at me. I'm the one who should be mad at him—and I am!"

Freddie grabbed Christopher's scarf to get his attention. "Christopher, it was an *accident*. Ted really didn't mean to do it. He could have hurt himself hitting that tree. You don't think he did it on purpose, do you?"

"No, of course not. But he should have been more careful!"

All afternoon Christopher kept thinking about the scratch on his new sled. Every time he looked at his sled, he became angrier at Ted. He was so angry he couldn't even enjoy sledding.

Later, one of Christopher's friends came running up the hill. "Christopher, come quickly! Ted

and Sed have been in an accident!"

"Where?" asked Christopher.

"The bottom of the hill. They crashed into that tree again. Sed's all right, but Ted's hurt. He keeps moaning and groaning and holding his leg. We don't know what to do."

Christopher looked at Freddie and started to speak, but Freddie said,

"Come on, Chris. There's no time to lose. Ted's hurt and needs our help." With that, Freddie jumped on the sled. Christopher hesitated.

"Come on, Chris! Ted's hurt!" shouted Freddie.

Christopher still hesitated. He just couldn't forget what Ted had done to his sled. He was still angry.

15

Finally, Freddie grabbed Christopher's scarf and pulled his friend onto the sled. "We're going. Ted needs us!" With that, they zoomed to the bottom of the hill.

They saw Sed sitting against a tree, looking white and shaken. A little bit farther away Ted sat with a lot of mice children standing around him.

Christopher got off his sled and walked over with Freddie. When he knelt to look at Ted, he suddenly forgot about being angry. Ted was his cousin, and he needed help.

"Where does it hurt, Ted?"

"It's my leg, Christopher.
I think it's broken."

"That's bad."

"How can we get him back to the
church?" asked one of the Church-
mice. "We can't carry him. He's
too heavy."

Christopher spoke up. "I know
how we can get him back. Freddie,
please bring my sled over here."

Freddie got the sled and
pulled it over.

17

"All right now, Ted. We're going to lift you onto the sled," Chris said. "Just take it easy. We'll put a tight bandage on your leg so it won't hurt so much."

Several of the mice boys lifted Ted slowly while Christopher held his leg straight. Taking a matchstick ski and a scarf someone gave him, Christopher tied Ted's leg carefully to the ski. Then Christopher took off his coat and covered him up. Taking off his scarf he put it underneath Ted's head so that he wouldn't bounce so much.

"All right now, Freddie, you pull him. I'm going to walk beside him and try to keep his leg from bouncing around."

Slowly the mice children took Ted back to the church.

"Now what do we do?" asked Freddie. "How can we get him into the church?"

The mice usually squeezed through a small hole in the church wall. "The only way is through the coal slide."

Christopher knew a lot about the furnace room where Tuffy the cat lived. He knew that one of the windows had a slide in it that was used to roll the coal down into the furnace room. Chris also knew the janitor usually left the window open for the coal man. If the mice could just get the sled to the slide, then they could push it down the slide and into the church basement.

The mice children got busy and built up a hill of snow which led right up to the window that had the coal slide.

In no time at all they had Ted safely down the slide and into the basement. From there several of the mice carried him to his home. Christopher took his coat, scarf, and sled and trudged wearily home with Freddie.

"Christopher," said Freddie, "I'm proud of you."

"You are?" asked Christopher in surprise. "Why is that, Freddie?"

"I'm just glad you're my friend," said Freddie. "I felt so proud of the way you helped Ted. It was really kind of you to take care of him and to use your sled to bring him home, after the way he scratched it and all."

"Yeah, well," said Christopher, "I'm pretty ashamed of the way I acted toward him. I asked him to forgive me."

"You did?" said Freddie. "What did he say?"

"He said he would. Then he thanked me for helping him. He's really a good mouse, you know, Freddie."

Later that night when Papa Churchmouse was tucking Christopher into bed he said, "Christopher, I heard about what happened today. I'm so pleased that when Ted really needed you, you forgave him, forgot your quarrel, and helped him."

"Papa, I remembered what I heard at Sunday School about quarreling," said Christopher.

"The teacher told us that the Bible says when we have a quarrel, we should forgive each other. That's what I tried to do."

"I think you did a wonderful thing," said Papa, pulling the covers up snuggly. "Quarreling doesn't help any of us. I'm so glad you're my son," he said, giving him a kiss on the cheek.

"I'm glad you're my papa too," murmured Christopher as he snuggled down for a well-deserved sleep.

DISCUSSION STARTERS

1. What did Christopher have that was brand-new?
2. Who wanted to borrow Christopher's sled?
3. Do you think Christopher should have loaned it to him? Why or why not?
4. How did Christopher react when Ted had the accident?
5. Do you think it was hard for Christopher to forgive Ted? What does the Scripture verse about forgiveness (Colossians 3:13) tell us to do when we have a quarrel with someone?